America, My Country
American Heroes

George Washington Carver

By Doraine Bennett

Clarke C. Scott, M.A.
Content Consultant

STATE STANDARDS PUBLISHING®

Your State • Your Standards • Your Grade Level

Dear Educators, Librarians and Parents . . .

Thank you for choosing books from State Standards Publishing! This book supports state Departments of Educations' standards for elementary level social studies and has been measured by the ATOS Readability Formula for Books (Accelerated Reader), the Lexile Framework for Reading, and the Fountas & Pinnell Benchmark Assessment System for Guided Reading. Photographs and/or illustrations, captions, and other design elements have been included to provide supportive visual messaging to enhance text comprehension. Glossary and Word Index sections introduce key new words and help young readers develop skills in locating and combining information. "Think With Bagster" questions provide teachers and parents with tools for additional learning activities and critical thinking development. We wish you all success in using this book to meet your student or child's learning needs.

Jill Ward, President

Publisher

State Standards Publishing, LLC
1788 Quail Hollow
Hamilton, GA 31811
USA
1.866.740.3056
www.statestandardspublishing.com

Library of Congress Control Number: 2011931734

ISBN-13: 978-1-935884-37-8 (hardcover)
ISBN-13: 978-1-935884-46-0 (paperback)

Printed in the United States of America, North Mankato, Minnesota, August 2011, 060611.

1 2 3 4 5 - CG - 15 14 13 12 11

About the Author

Doraine Bennett has a degree in professional writing from Columbus State University in Columbus, Georgia, and has been writing and teaching writing for over twenty years. She is a published author of numerous books for children, as well as magazine articles for both children and adults. She is the editor of the National Infantry Association's *Infantry Bugler* magazine. Doraine enjoys reading and flower gardening. She lives in Georgia with her husband, Cliff.

About the Content Consultant

Clarke C. Scott holds degrees from Central Michigan University and has 31 years of experience as a classroom teacher, building principal and system-wide administrator. Clarke currently serves as Director of Middle School Education and Lead Director for History with Pittsylvania County Schools in Virginia. He enjoys hiking, kayaking, caving, and exploring Virginia's and our nation's history. He shares his adventures both above and underground with his wife, Joyce, and three grown children.

Table of Contents

George and the Slave Stealers 5

The Plant Doctor 7

George, the Student 9

George, the Teacher 11

Building a Lab 13

What About Peanuts? 15

No Waste 17

The Moving School 19

George, the Helper 21

Glossary 22

Word Index 23

Think With Bagster 24

Hi, I'm Bagster!
Let's learn about
American Heroes.

MY STATE

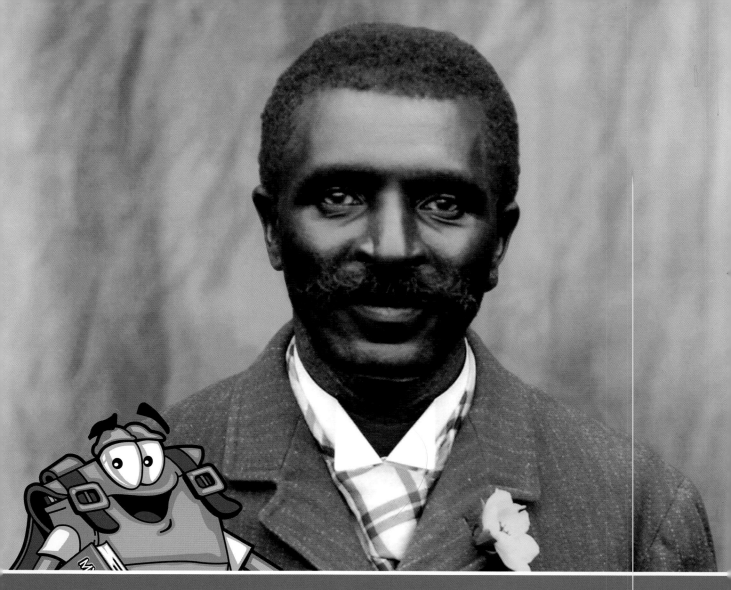

George Washington Carver was born in Missouri.

George and the Slave Stealers

George Washington Carver was born in Missouri. His mother was a **slave**. George was a slave, too. Moses and Susan Carver were their owners. People owned slaves. This was called **slavery**. One day bad men stole George and his mother. George was found. But his mother was never seen again.

George took care of the garden, like this boy.

Time Line

About 1864
Born

1865
Slavery ends

The Plant Doctor

America fought a war. The war ended slavery. George was free. Moses and Susan raised George. They were kind to him. Susan taught him to read. George was sick a lot. So he worked in the kitchen with Susan. He learned to cook. He took care of the garden. George loved plants. People called him the *plant doctor*.

George went to a school for African Americans.

Time Line

About 1864
Born

1865
Slavery ends

1890
Studies art

George, the Student

George could not go to school with white children. He went to a school for African Americans. It was far from home. George had to move. Later George wanted to study art. But the school was for white students. So he went to school in Iowa. He liked drawing and painting. He liked to sew and knit, too. He made things for his friends.

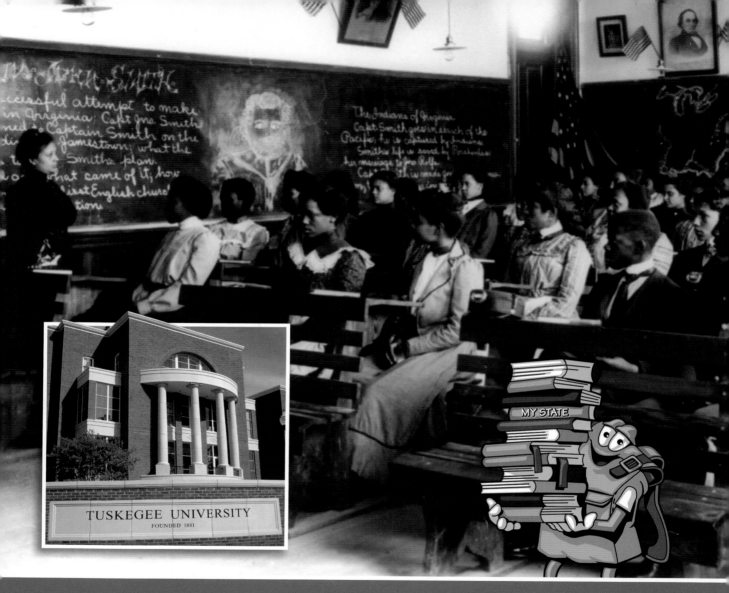

George went to Tuskegee Institute.

TUSKEGEE UNIVERSITY
FOUNDED 1881

MY STATE

Time Line

About 1864
Born

1865
Slavery ends

1890
Studies art

George, the Teacher

George still loved nature. He studied farming. George became a scientist. He learned all about plants. Booker T. Washington had a school in Alabama. It was called Tuskegee Institute. It was a school for African American students. Booker asked George to be a teacher. George and Booker wanted to help poor people have better lives.

George and his students built a lab.

Time Line

About 1864
Born

1865
Slavery ends

1890
Studies art

Building a Lab

George studied **crops** and soil. Crops are plants that are grown for food. But the school was small. George did not have a **lab**. He needed a place to try out his ideas. George and his students found old jars. They found pots and pans. They took string and wire from the trash. George showed the students what to do. They built a lab.

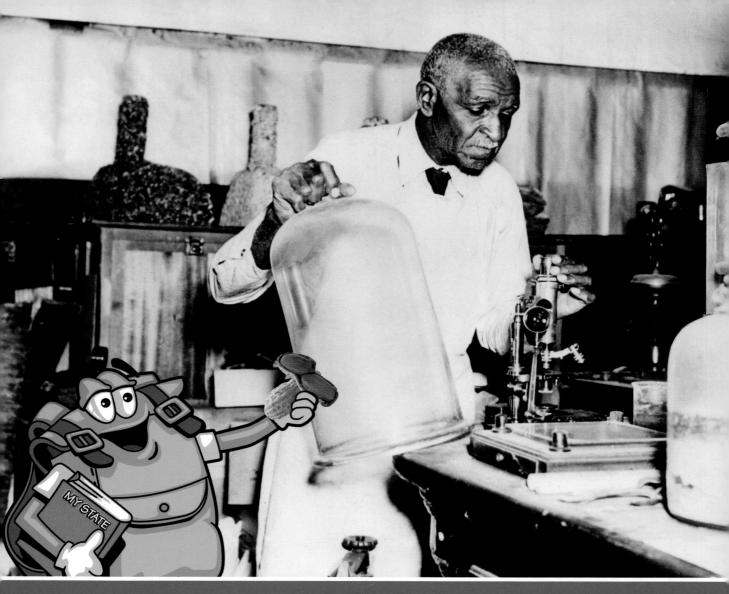

George found over 300 ways to use peanuts.

Time Line

About 1864
Born

1865
Slavery ends

1890
Studies art

What About Peanuts?

George tried his new ideas with farmers. He said, "Grow peanuts one year. Grow cotton the next year." Changing crops helped the soil. But what would they do with all those peanuts? No one knew. George found over 300 ways to use peanuts. He made peanut milk and peanut paper. He made peanut soap. He even made cheese.

George studied sweet potatoes, too.

Time Line

About 1864
Born

1865
Slavery ends

1890
Studies art

No Waste

George studied sweet potatoes, too. He found lots of ways to use them. He made candy. He made flour for cooking. He made paint. He made sweet potato pie. George used things most people threw away. Nature did not waste anything. People should not waste things. That is what George thought.

George took the school to farms.

Time Line

About 1864	**1865**	**1890**
Born	Slavery ends	Studies art

The Moving School

George built a moving school. He took the school to farms. He took it to churches and other schools. He taught people to eat better food. He taught farmers to grow better crops. He taught them new ways to care for animals.

George loved nature. He changed farming.

Time Line

About 1864
Born

1865
Slavery ends

1890
Studies art

George, the Helper

George always wore a flower on his coat.
He loved nature all his life. He believed
God made all of nature. His belief made
him a good helper to people. George
died in 1943. He changed farming. He
changed the way poor
people lived, too.

1896
Goes to Tuskegee

1897
Starts moving school

1943
Dies

21

Glossary

crops – Plants that are grown for food.

lab – A room where scientists test things or try out new ideas.

slave – A person who is owned by another person. Slaves are made to work against their will.

slavery – A system where people own other people.

Word Index

African Americans, 9, 11

art, 9

Carver, Moses and Susan, 5, 7

crops, 13, 15, 19

farmers, 15, 19

farming, 11, 21

lab, 13

nature, 11, 17, 21

peanuts, 15

plant doctor, 7

plants, 7, 11, 19

school, 9, 11, 13, 19

scientist, 11

slave, 5

slavery, 5, 7

sweet potatoes, 17

Tuskegee Institute, 11

Washington, Booker T., 11

Editorial Credits

Designer: Michael Sellner, Corporate Graphics, North Mankato, Minnesota
Consultant/Marketing Design: Alison Hagler, Basset and Becker Advertising, Columbus, Georgia

Image Credits – *All images © copyright contributor below unless otherwise specified.*

Cover – JVPD/ImageEnvision. **4/5** – JVPD/Image Envision. **6/7** – Jeff Greenberg/Alamy. **8/9** – North Wind Picture Archives. **10/11** – Classroom: US Library of Congress, Frances Benjamin Johnson/Wikipedia; Tuskegee: Andre Jenny/Alamy. **12/13** – New York Public Library/Africana & Black History/Schomburg Center for Research in Black Culture/General Research and Reference Division. **14/15** – Lab: New York Public Library/Africana & Black History/Schomburg Center for Research in Black Culture/General Research and Reference Division; Peanuts: Georgi Georgiev/iStockphoto. **16/17** – Field: New York Public Library/Africana & Black History/Schomburg Center for Research in Black Culture/General Research and Reference Division; Potatoes: Floortje/iStockphoto. **18/19** – New York Public Library/Africana & Black History/Schomburg Center for Research in Black Culture/General Research and Reference Division. **20/21** – "George Washington Carver" painting courtesy George Washington Carver National Monument, Diamond, MO, © Paula Giltner, Joplin, MO.

Think With Bagster

1. George never wasted anything. Why? How can you be like George?

2. How do you know that George wanted to learn? What problems did he have? Do you think things are different today?

3. Why do you think George always wore a flower on his coat?

4. Why did George invent things from peanuts and sweet potatoes?